Spectacular SPOT WHAT!

Nick Bryant & Rowan Summers

hinkler

Elegant Penguins

Horse & Cart

Also available
in this series:
Spot What!
Spot What! Amazing
Spot What! Magical
Spot What! Metropolis
Spot What! Carnival

Published by Hinkler Books Pty Ltd
45-55 Fairchild Street,
Heatherton Victoria 3202 Australia
www.hinkler.com.au

hinkler

Authors: Nick Bryant and Rowan Summers
Cover design: Peter Tovey

ISBN: 978 1 8651 5916 4

Printed and bound in China

Sundial

Cello

Chequered Flag

Sewing Machine

Candelabra

Blimp

Contents

Animals	4
Blocks	6
Spectacles	8
Green	10
Underwater	12
Pipes	14
Sport	16
Jigsaw	18
Circus	20
Bouquet	22
Gravity	24
Fireworks	26
Extra Clues & Games	28
Spot What Challenge	29

Cuckoo Clock

Tyrannosaurus Rex

Can you spot two elephants,
Three giraffes and a bat,
A lion, a tiger, a leopard,
An owl and a pussycat?

Can you find four eagles,
Three dogs, a hippo, a moose,
A sheep, a mouse and a rabbit,
A golden egg and a goose?

SPECTACULAR GORGE ☞

5

Can you spot a rocking horse,
A piggy-bank, a lollipop,
A sewing machine, a tambourine,
A submarine, a spinning top?

Find a helicopter,
A scarecrow and a bee,
A jack, a train, a crown, a plane,
And the letters 'ABC'.

Can you spot a birthday cake,
A telephone, a ring,
A rattle and a thimble,
A ladybug, a wing?

Can you find a lobster,
An eyeball and a key,
A skier and an ice cube,
A log, a nest, a tree?

Shirtzen Paint

Can you spot a watering can,
A Christmas tree and a parrot,
A house, a lettuce, an olive,
A chameleon and a carrot?

Find two snakes and a tractor,
A horn and six crawling insects,
Three frogs, a four-leafed clover,
And a tyrannosaurus rex.

Can you spot a jellyfish,
A seahorse and two skulls,
A turtle and a lighthouse,
One pearl and two seagulls?

Find five leaping dolphins,
A crab, a pair of oars,
An octopus, a treasure chest,
A coin, a kettle, a door.

SS SPECTACULAR

FIZZO

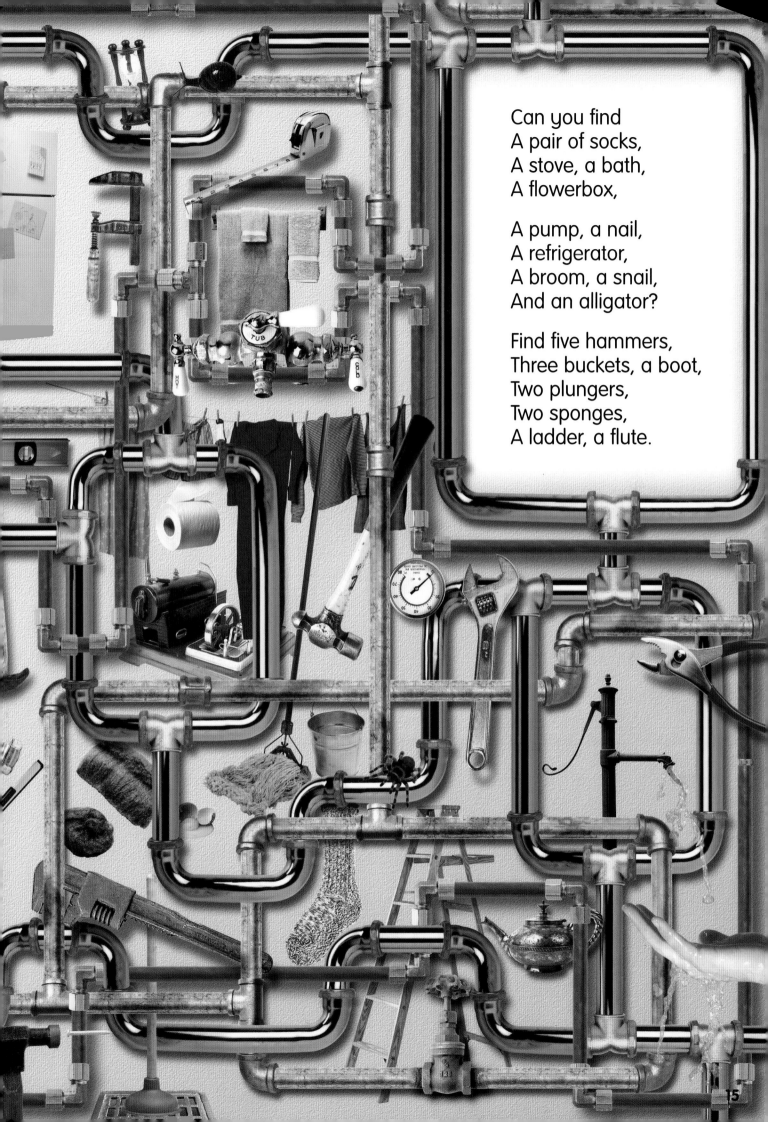

Can you find
A pair of socks,
A stove, a bath,
A flowerbox,

A pump, a nail,
A refrigerator,
A broom, a snail,
And an alligator?

Find five hammers,
Three buckets, a boot,
Two plungers,
Two sponges,
A ladder, a flute.

SPOT WHAT

Can you spot a basketball,
A tennis ball, two bats,
A skipping rope, a bowling ball,
A fisherman's hat?

Find a pair of ice skates,
Two whistles and a dart,
A stopwatch, a chequered flag,
A saddle, a horse and cart.

Can you find a scorpion,
A lizard and a truck,
A surfboard, a skateboard,
A blackboard and a duck?

Can you spot a windmill,
An astronaut, a car,
An eggshell, a footprint,
A statue, a guitar?

DINGELING BROS. CIRCUS

Roll Up! Roll Up!,
A spectacular to see,
The circus is in town,
Entertainment guaranteed!

Witness the high-flying
Fellini Brothers,
Perform death-defying,
Stupefying stunts above us,

With jugglers juggling,
Clowns clowning around,
The high wire dare-devils,
Dare-devillings astound,

A better time cannot
Be found anywhere,
So come on down,
To the Circus & Fair

KINDLY CONTROL YOURSELF

Frank Flemming's Fantastic Flea Circus

Can you spot a juggler,
Five stars and seven clowns,
A trapeze artist, a unicyclist,
A chimp and a merry-go-round,

A pair of tightrope walkers,
Three tumbling acrobats,
An apple, a pear, a balancing chair,
Three hoops and a very tall hat?

To the Fellini Brothers,

Can you spot a ball of wool,
A stapler and a fan,
A wagon wheel, a fishing reel,
An egg and frying pan?

Find a candelabra,
A knife, a fork and a pie,
A banjo and a compass,
An umbrella and bow tie.

Can you spot a wishing well,
A parachute, a polar bear,
A bird in a cage, an open page,
A witch and a rocking chair?

Find a worm and a cuckoo clock,
A brush, a comb and a cello,
Two balloons, a shovel, a spoon,
And five little flowers of yellow.

25

Can you spot a jack-in-the-box,
A peacock and a dragon,
A pirate and a rooster,
A ship, a mermaid, a wagon?

Find a hummingbird, a harp,
A unicorn, a kite,
A bucking bronco, a grand piano,
The name of a day and a knight.

SPECTACULAR

See if you can spot these things in every picture:

Can you find the words SPOT WHAT,
The number ten, a gnome,
A butterfly, an hourglass,
And an ice-cream cone?

Rocket

Submarine

Rules For The Spot What Game

1. Flip a coin to see who goes first. The winner of the coin toss is 'the caller' and the other player is 'the spotter'.

2. The caller chooses a page from the book and picks an item for the spotter to find, saying, for example, 'Can you spot a submarine?'

3. The spotter must then try to find the item.

4. If the spotter can't find it, the caller gets 5 points and shows the spotter where it is and has another turn.

5. If the spotter can find the item, then he or she gets 5 points and now it's his or her turn to be the caller.

6. The first to reach 30 points wins but you could also set your own limit or simply play best out of three!

You can make the game more challenging by putting a time limit of one to three minutes on each search. Try making up your own games too!

Chameleon

Olive

The Spot What Challenge.

The following items are much harder to find so get ready for the challenge.

Jack

Tuning Fork

Animals
(page 4/5)

A frog
3 wise monkeys
3 lizards
2 feathers
Early bird gets worm
A spider and a fly
A snail

Spectacles
(page 8/9)

A diamond
A rhinoceros
A lightbulb
A fish bowl
9 marbles
A mirror
A jack

Witch

Blocks
(page 6/7)

9 balloons
A horn
A kettle
5 chess pieces
A piano
A coin
A star

Green
(page 10/11)

A circuit board
A leprechaun
Sunglasses
A brussel sprout
A watermelon
A window
10 green bottles

Astronaut

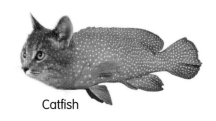
Catfish

Ice-cream Cone

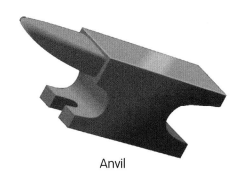

Anvil

Underwater
(page 12/13)

A catfish and a dogfish
4 starfish
4 scuba divers
A seal
2 anchors
A message in a bottle
7 seashells

Sport
(page 16/17)

A yo-yo
A hockey puck
5 soccer balls
A boomerang
2 catcher's mitts
2 shuttlecocks
2 pairs of binoculars

Scarecrow

Pipes
(page 14/15)

A teapot
5 toilet rolls
An egg
A coat hanger
A fire hydrant
A toilet brush
A set of plans

Jigsaw
(page 18/19)

10 gold bars
A wind-up mouse
A pair of scissors
A jet plane
A London bus
Chinese checkers
A match

Flea Circus

Merry-go-round

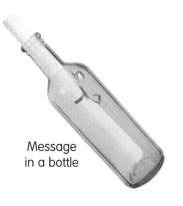

Message
in a bottle

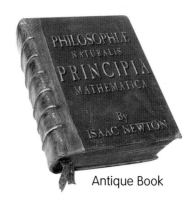

Antique Book

Circus
(page 20/21)

2 photographers
3 noisemakers
6 umbrellas
Comedy and Tragedy
2 elephants
A snake
2 elegant penguins

Gravity
(page 24/25)

A kitten
A dragonfly
The Mona Lisa
Time flies
East and west
The alphabet
A butter churn

Butterfly

Bouquet
(page 22/23)

A ships wheel
An elephant
A gramophone
A fluffy bunny
A pair of ballet shoes
A guitar
A swan

Fireworks
(page 26/27)

The Pied Piper
A fish
A bow and arrow
A bridge
A fairy
A skipping girl
A court jester

Gnome

Dogfish

Trapeze
Artist

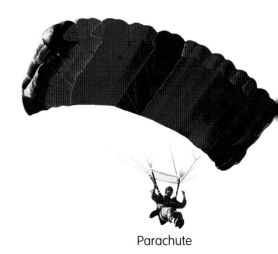

Parachute

Hourglass

Acknowledgements

We would like to thank the following people:

Sam Bryant
Sam Grimmer
Peter Tovey Studios
Qi Crystals Fossils Minerals, Melbourne, VIC
Suzanne Buckley
Samantha Boardman
Sante Cigany
Clare Tennant
Dingeling Bros Circus
Everyone at Hinkler Books

**Backgrounds for 'Gravity' and 'Circus'
by Stephen Evans
s_evans42@yahoo.com**

Horn

Four-leafed Clover

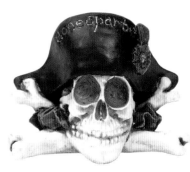

Skull